INVESTIGATING MYSTERIOUS PLACES

STONEHENGE
MONUMENT OF MYSTERY

by Scott Sonneborn

CAPSTONE PRESS
a capstone imprint

Published by Capstone Press, an imprint of Capstone
1710 Roe Crest Drive, North Mankato, Minnesota 56003
capstonepub.com

Copyright © 2025 by Capstone. All rights reserved. No part of this publication may be reproduced in whole or in part, or stored in a retrieval system, or transmitted in any form or by any means, electronic, mechanical, photocopying, recording, or otherwise, without written permission of the publisher.

Library of Congress Cataloging-in-Publication Data is available on the Library of Congress website.

ISBN: 9781669093657 (hardcover)
ISBN: 9781669093602 (paperback)
ISBN: 9781669093619 (ebook PDF)

Summary: Travel to Stonehenge and discover the secrets of this ancient stone monument! How were these massive stones transported and set upright using only the tools of early humans? This book explores the possible purposes of the so-called Monument of Mystery—from space observatory to sacred burial ground—and examines the latest research and theories about the fascinating structure.

Editorial Credits
Editor: Donald Lemke; Designer: Tracy Davies; Media Researcher: Svetlana Zhurkin; Production Specialist: Katy LaVigne

Image Credits
Alamy: Heritage Image Partnership Ltd, 6, Maurice Savage, 24; Bridgeman Images: From the British Library Archive, 13; Dreamstime: Chimeandsense, 26, IanBushwacker, 15; Getty Images: Captain Skyhigh, 5, Dorling Kindersley, 14, duncan1890, 27, rolikett, 29; Newscom: Heritage Images/English Heritage, 23; Shutterstock: Aliaksei Hintau (smoke background), 2 and throughout, Art studio G (Stonehenge icon), cover and throughout, George W. Bailey, 19, Kevin Standage, 21, monmii, cover, Nicholas Grey, 17, Peter Hermes Furian, 11, Phil Harland, 10, PTZ Pictures, 18, Rob Follett Creative, 20, Victor Maschek, 7; SuperStock: DeAgostini, 9, 25, Mary Evans Picture Library, 12

Any additional websites and resources referenced in this book are not maintained, authorized, or sponsored by Capstone. All product and company names are trademarks™ or registered® trademarks of their respective holders.

TABLE OF CONTENTS

Chapter One
ANCIENT MONUMENT.. 4

Chapter Two
HOW WAS STONEHENGE BUILT? 8

Chapter Three
STONEHENGE OVER TIME..16

Chapter Four
UNSOLVED MYSTERIES 22

GLOSSARY..30
READ MORE 31
INTERNET SITES...31
INDEX 32
ABOUT THE AUTHOR..32

Chapter One

ANCIENT MONUMENT

Stonehenge is one of the most **mysterious** places on Earth. The **monument** is a circle of almost 100 giant stone blocks. Many of the stones stand in pairs. A third stone often rests across the top of the pairs.

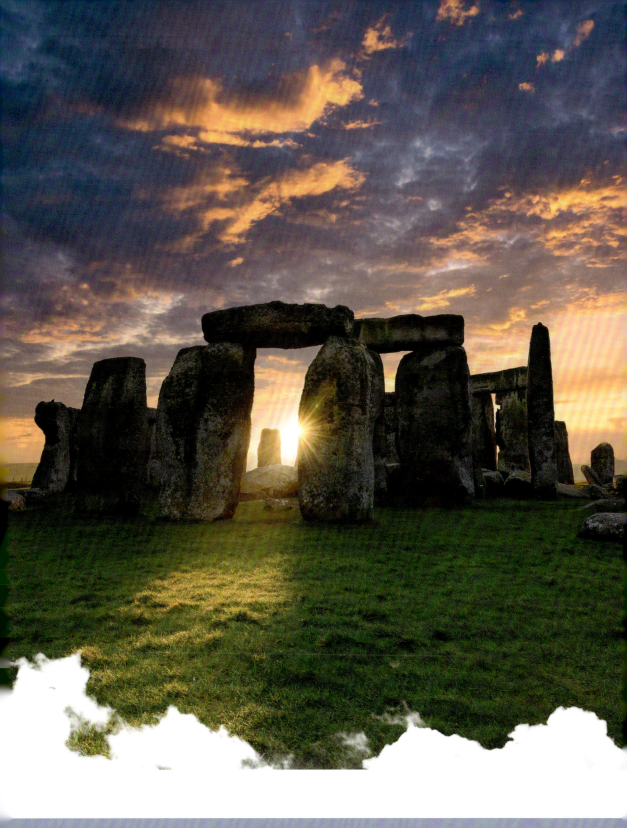

Stonehenge was built on an empty **plain** in England. It is very old. Work on the monument started about 5,000 years ago. It took more than 1,000 years to build.

Teams of workers putting up the Stonehenge circle

Tourists walk next to the Stonehenge monument.

Ever since, people have wondered who built Stonehenge and why. Today, nearly one million people visit the site every year to explore its many mysteries.

FACT

The Stonehenge monument is 500 years older than the oldest pyramids in Egypt!

Chapter Two

HOW WAS STONEHENGE BUILT?

Some of the stone blocks are sarsen, a kind of rock found nearby. Some of the sarsen stones weigh 40 tons (36.3 metric tons). They are more than 20 feet (6 meters) tall. Experts think moving each block took hundreds of people.

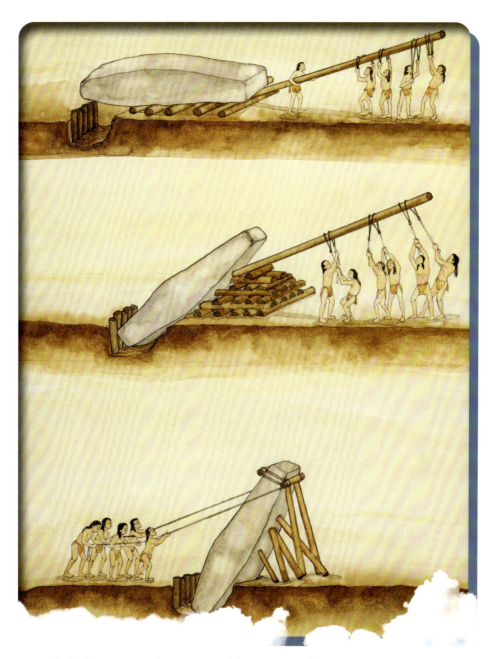

Workers may have used levers and ropes to place the giant stones.

A rocky summit in the Preseli Hills

Other parts of Stonehenge are made of bluestone from the Preseli Hills. These hills are 150 miles (241 kilometers) away from the site.

The people who built Stonehenge did not have wheels or metal tools. How could they have moved such heavy stones? It seems nearly impossible!

Many people worked together to move and place the stones.

FACT

In 1986, Stonehenge became a World Heritage Site to honor and protect its history.

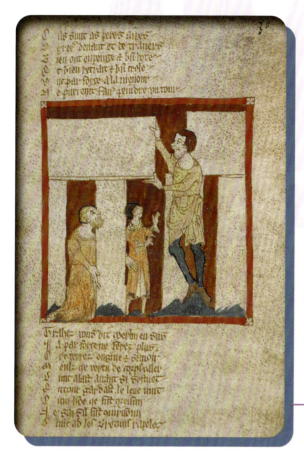

A medieval book illustration showing Merlin (center) using magic to help build Stonehenge

For hundreds of years, people believed a wizard named Merlin moved the stones. In one famous story, Merlin used his magic to make the stones light enough for one person to carry.

13

Today, historians and **archaeologists** who have studied Stonehenge have other answers. They think **ancient** people tied the giant stones to wooden sleds.

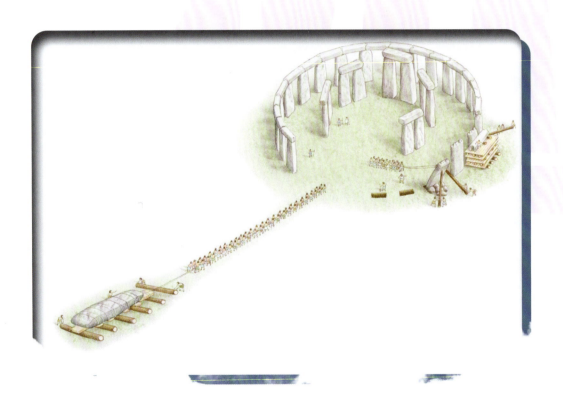

Prehistoric workers pull a giant stone using ropes and logs.

The River Avon may have been used to transport stones to the site.

The sleds allowed people to drag the stones down from the hills. Then people put the stones on rafts. They floated the stones on rivers the rest of the way.

Chapter Three

STONEHENGE OVER TIME

Stonehenge has changed a lot throughout its 5,000-year history. During its **construction**, the builders moved the stone blocks around several times.

Stonehenge monument seen from above

More recently, many of the stones were taken away and used to build other things. Today, there are 43 bluestones in the inner circle. Experts believe the site originally had twice as many.

Some bluestones forming Stonehenge's inner circle

The original appearance of Stonehenge

In the outer circle, 50 sarsen stones still stand. But 3,000 years ago, there were many more of them.

Church Henge is a well-preserved henge in Knowlton, England.

Still, Stonehenge today looks a lot like it did when it was built. Other henges, or circular structures, weren't so lucky.

That's why it took a while to discover that Stonehenge isn't the only henge. There are others nearby that are older and larger.

The stone circle within Avebury Henge is the largest stone circle in Great Britain.

Chapter Four

UNSOLVED MYSTERIES

The builders who created Stonehenge didn't know how to read or write. They left no written records to tell us why they made Stonehenge or how they used the monument.

From the beginning, Stonehenge may have been connected to prehistoric burial practices.

Historians do know some things for sure. Stonehenge was definitely a **cemetery**. Hundreds of graves have been found there.

Human remains from a burial site near Stonehenge displayed at a museum

FACT

Archeologists know that many men, women, and children were buried at Stonehenge in the late Neolithic period, more than 5,000 years ago.

Aligned with the sun's position during the summer and winter solstices, Stonehenge might have been used to track the solar year.

Some historians think Stonehenge might also have been a giant calendar.

One of the stones is in a special spot. On the longest day of the year, the sun rises over it. On the shortest day of the year, the sun sets over this stone. Because of this, some archaeologists think that Stonehenge might have been a place where people **worshipped** the sun.

Visitors watch the summer solstice sunrise at Stonehenge.

A large celebration taking place at Stonehenge

We may not know exactly what the ancient people who built Stonehenge did there. But we do know that for a thousand years, large numbers of them visited Stonehenge.

But then, about 3,000 years ago, they stopped. No one knows why. It's another of the mysteries of Stonehenge we may never solve.

Glossary

ancient (AYN-shuhnt)—very old, from a long time ago

archaeologist (ar-kee-OL-uh-jist)—a scientist who studies old things left by people from the past to learn how they lived

cemetery (SEM-uh-ter-ee)—a place where dead bodies are buried

construction (kuhn-STRUHK-shuhn)—the process of building or making something

monument (MAHN-yuh-ment)—a building, pillar, stone, or statue honoring a person or an event

mysterious (mis-TEER-ee-uhs)—things that are difficult or impossible to explain or understand

plain (PLAYN)—a broad area of level or rolling treeless country

worship (WUR-ship)—show honor, respect, and love for a god or deity, often through prayers, rituals, or ceremonies

Read More

Dickmann, Nancy. *Your Passport to England.* North Mankato, MN: Capstone, 2022.

Omoth, Tyler. *Handbook to Stonehenge, the Bermuda Triangle, and Other Mysterious Locations.* North Mankato, MN: Capstone, 2018.

Weitzman, Elizabeth. *Mysteries of Stonehenge.* Minneapolis: Lerner Publications, 2018.

Internet Sites

BBC: What Is Stonehenge?
bbc.co.uk/bitesize/articles/zqd496f#zjd496f

History: Stonehenge
history.com/topics/european-history/stonehenge

National Geographic Kids: Stonehenge Facts!
natgeokids.com/uk/discover/history/general-history/stonehenge-facts

Index

age, 6, 16, 19, 28
ancient people, 14, 27
archaeologists, 14, 26

beliefs, 13, 26
bluestone, 10, 18

calendar, 25
cemetery, 24
construction, 6, 8, 12, 14–15, 16

England, 6, 20

henges, 20

Merlin, 13

Preseli Hills, 10

sarsen, 8, 19
stones, 4, 8, 14, 16, 21, 26
  number of , 4, 18–19
  size of, 8
  transportation of, 13, 14–15
  types of, 8, 10
sun, 26

tourism, 7, 27

About the Author

Scott Sonneborn is the author of more than 40 books for kids. He's also written a bunch of TV shows and been nominated for both an Emmy and a Hugo Award. He lives in Los Angeles with his wife and their two sons.